SATURN
RETURNS

New York City

SATURN RETURNS

Charline Tetiyevsky

In honor of us all soaring high-speed on this beloved rock
without burning up.

Cover Image: Charline Tetiyevsky
Title Image and Interior Images: National
Aeronautics and Space Administration
Author Photo: David Diperstein

Printed in the United States of America
First Edition: March 2023
ISBN: 979-8-9861950-0-1

Acknowledgements:
"The Night After Mario Richards Forgot Who He Was, Who His
Father Was, That His Mother, Before She Died, Had Always Told
Him to Stay off the Kitchen Counter"
First published in *Quarto*

Printed by Potato Chip, LLC
New York City

potatochip.nyc

Contents

Storm on the Pole

Prometheus Set a Forest Fire

♄

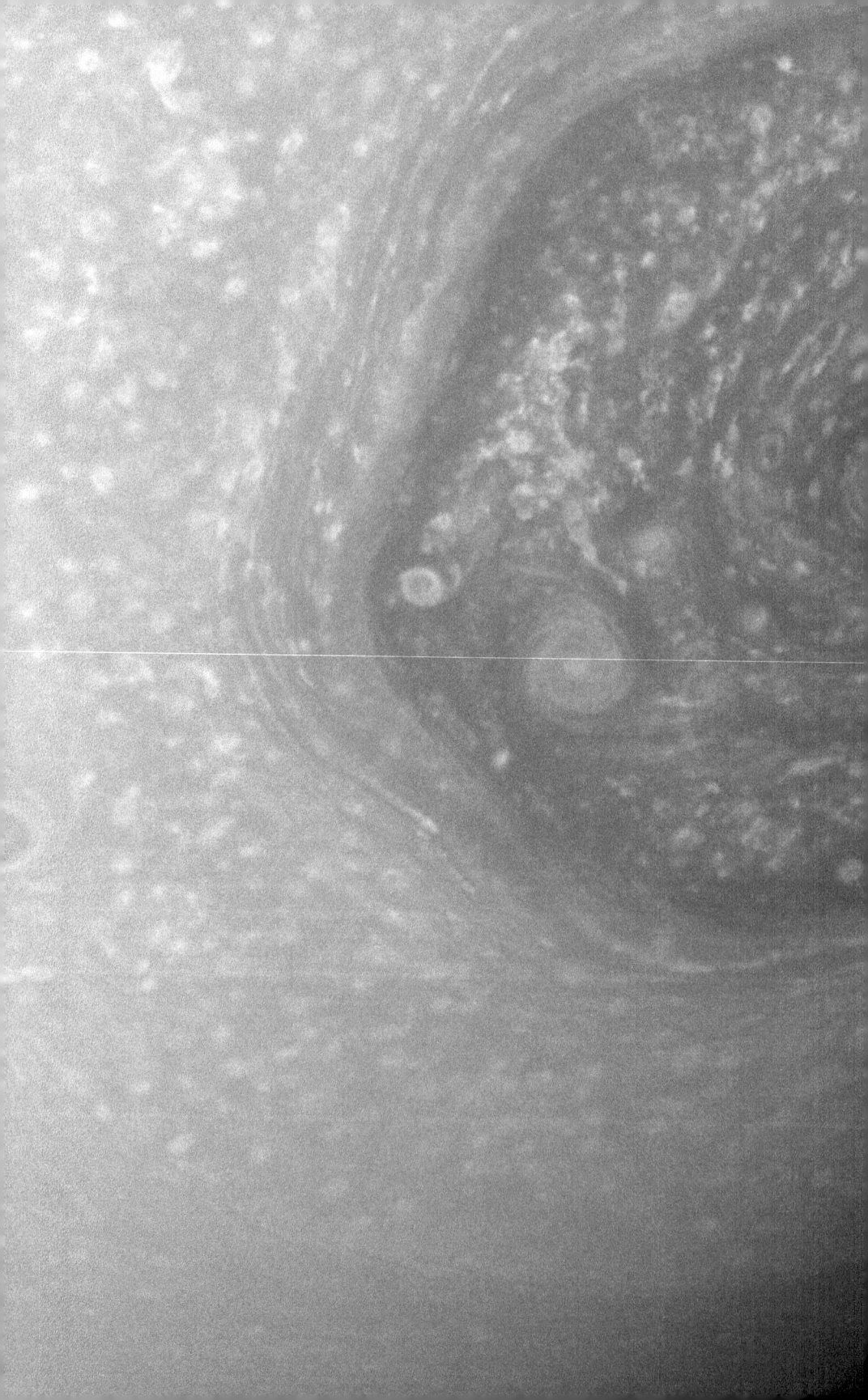

STORM
ON THE POLE

Happy birthday,
if you believe the old stories about the sky:

Saturn whirls around the sun upon its even-keeled disc every ten thousand seven hundred and fifty six days so why is it when almost thirty years after the day you were born he returns to the gates to greet the worn silk of his throne, his crown gilded and mouth full of blood, sonless, they say this means victory? I say it is Pyrrhus' they say yes, they say *Congratulations! You won!* I say but this means something like a dog forever chasing its tail, something like the sign painted welcome to adulthood, like welcome to trying to straighten the orbit that bends into itself.

He fell in the morning, like Icarus

I have
disparaged the name, I have
not wanted to learn to spell it at all,
so many vowels and stutterings,
phonemes trying to speak words evasive, I have felt like that,

I have felt that I am not worthy of speech,
that I am not whole unless
fractured, that I am not enough anymore to say
what I do with any meaning.

I fill my body
with thoughts of the decades-deceased,
with the ways I've been done wrong, I think

about how I've been held
in the mornings, like being brushed for school
while I slept through knots pulled
from my hair; I can sleep through anything
when I want to get away.

I fear that I have not honored
this body, that I do not love living like everyone else
and so it will be taken from me
now that I have only just landed.

I've seen it, I've seen such games
where the breath is pulled from under you

so fast, like the man who flew down from the roof past my window, Icarus still winged but on a voyage to the bright morning concrete, in New York where every sparkling sidewalk can look just like the sun.

The Night After Mario Richards Forgot Who He Was, Who His Father Was, That His Mother, Before She Died, Had Always Told Him to Stay Off the Kitchen Counter

He's convinced: the staccato whine that manifests itself in his lower bowels after he fucks on Momma's Formica is just another way to say: once, I loved.

What good is memory if it isn't visceral?

Girl's unfazed; she's smelled worse and she's got things to snort and cutlery to steal and he just lets her because whose house is this anyway? Good thing Mario knows how to force a lock because he's got no keys, it's not his lock, he swears to himself on his mother's grave because somewhere deep down in the recesses of his reptilian brain the one thing he's certain of is that she's dead.

Cokehead says she's impressed by the granite countertops and crosses her scabbed legs, alabaster against the flecks and marbled veins.

Nobody's home to hear the sound of her laugh. Walls sunburnt but for picture frame-sized squares remind Mario's father of loss so he's off in Boca, counting crushed pebbles and making eyes at varicose legs. Maybe the brochures were right when they called this place the Jewel at the Gates of Heaven and maybe Mario's mother is on this beach that's covered in resorts covered in caramel wrappers.

Grief makes one hell of an opener. Drunk off of margaritas too strong on the salty rim, he considers bikinis with dots on them, ocean foam. The sunscreen says "expired, don't you do it," but he just squeezes a thick line of white onto his chest and rubs and doesn't question the sting.

Cokehead crushes her little baggie with that card from Mario's wallet that was declined at the bar and he doesn't care that she pushes his lips aside to rub what's left on his gums. When her Parliament crackles alive the light makes her look like Momma Mary.

Mario is no daddy. He is the hero of his own story and he does not need a father, nobody needs a father, he says aloud. On the table he's got all the things he needs: his wallet and his keys, a box of rubbers and forgotten plans for baking a cake. He's got eyes for silk window treatments and a wall-mounted pair of bronzed shoes, he's got the feeling that somewhere behind the television there is a mechanism that tells the sprinkler when not to run. And he's got the taste, Cokehead says mid-sunrise, of mourning on his tongue.

Once, I was far away from home

In every fable,
the most sought reward: feast.
I know I am sane again
because I binge on chocolate,
on chips, on chicken salt—
did you know we don't have chicken salt back home?
did you know back home we had everything and nothing?
what a sight to behold, so burdened with opulence.
did you know I only call places home now
out of habit because
home is a place where you put your feet up
and these are all places where I still must run.
I spend my time saying
things were like this but now they're like that
like some morbid corpse,
I say that now to seem young but
I am young
did you know I don't feel young
did you know that being young is
pretending not to know you're going to die,
that happiness is a willful deception,
a feast in famine.

In the name of the return to Saturn

I too have consumed those closest to me
head first, have been wronged and wrongest
spilled blood I loved on my own blouse to avoid the curse,
led myself to the gallows and dropped below the floor.

I've stuck with a man who uses saline drops
when he doesn't have salt; find yourself a man who
   a man who will always call you by the name you chose.

I've lived staked into the irradiated soil, burnt off the soles of my feet
so I couldn't stand. Carried my own mistakes
like a dirge stuck in the ear-space, on repeat ad infinitum
   ad infinitum, at the minimum the costs paid were always more
         than I could spare.

Extinguished

I once loved a man who killed a dog.
I relapsed on him last night in a dream,
with my head in the hood of my jacket
and seawater in my eyes
at 30,000 feet.

I've been staying celibate
and I've been staying sober
and I have cleaned my aura
with the softest of golds, mended what has
been broken and then prayed over,
crazy glued crazy back into
a shatter-proof marble block.

Can you see in my face
that I've always never wanted
to be here, that I thought I could
handle being spilled across the floor
over and over again, let myself
be and get spun so thin
that my fibers split?

Haven't I ever told you
I only ever wanted
to be loved
by destruction?

Code in Triage

Eras of errors
hang off of me like bloodletting cows,
and I have taken on the superstitions of my forbearers:
knock on the wooden bedpost to wake up someone else.

Thinking about
the years I spent buried inside
my own hands, it's like falling down the deepest hole.

But I have searched the volcano,
and I have baptized myself in its waters.

Anyone else could've found me in my own shrinking body,
like the part of a bomb that doesn't disappear,
like shrapnel: embedded.

Burn the harvest

Howling absurdities strung across two people bound together
with the pinkest of bows, the prettiest of finishes. Affection polished
and reflective, a showman's sword with no hilt:
I can bleed in the three-ring onto my own blackened shoes.

We drunkenly orate in our good clothes
about how "when two people grow together,"
but not about what happens
when they stretch apart in a diagonal.

There are no speeches given
for an unworn dress and a veil lost
in the garment bag,
for those who sliced open their whole palms simply trying to get a grip.

Warning Label

If your hands multiply,
If you discover the people you love have all turned to what:
Do not be alarmed when the horizon collapses.
If the seas curdle,
the grasses immolate. Do not be alarmed if
the gorges slough off into the riverbed and dam up the creek.
Do not be alarmed if the sky molds and rains down spores
upon you that stick and grow blue fur on your back. Do not
be alarmed that you didn't do the dishes before the apocalypse,
turn the oven off before the reign of the goat man,
get your terminal degree before the sun exploded,
do not be alarmed, don't bother,
you don't even know better
than to not step foot-first into the smoldering chasm.

This is a poem about the bad l*ve

we were not saved by the grace of beauty, and like the other
fineries of this world you have largely not touched my palms.

I would do anyone
for a poor man's reenactment
of what I imagined we once had.

in these choleric times I dry heave upon love,
peristalsis to keep my thoughts down in this
borrowed corpse.

This is a poem for anyone who's had to wash their hand
clean of its ring.

to seek wholeness from psychic entanglement,
what fools we had been.

When atoms split they explode like we did,
destroyed along with the landscape we'd tilled and dug
and planted sunflowers in.

Fallen

that fear is weak: grecian, classical—
the body meant instead to blindly charge forth into death,
relinquish the bones, the will,
hopes like robes, slipping off shoulders like skin.
We must like fruit die for the seeds in our bellies—

to all, it seems, but us
divine is the creation,
detestful the breakdown.

Mermaid

Drunk,
Gerald Martin was so drunk he couldn't tell what had hit his boat,
covered in red algae and barely afloat—but for lips
who matched the water below, a spillable egg, an unhatchable yolk.

Behold! He says: The hands that drifted slowly slipped
soundlessly against the hull and so she emerged a swell,
slick with questions. The way Gerald told it, he swore
he could hear just one pickled cough come from her chest.

But it was late;
dinner had to be on the plate.
Gerald floated home to the horizon, an unwavering eye
upon his prized catch.

Rigor Mortis (Memento Mori for the Grotesque)

True, that the sworling charred masses gasped after the apocalypse: we licked ourselves clean of the fragments of the pestilent life that rained from the sky like pesticides. Our tongues made us divine, stripped the taut cauls of rebirth away from our flesh newly marbled with blood a vertebrae at a time. Slowly we fused against one another, moans the marrow that strung us together and intertwined broken arms, twisting together the veins that pulsed, the veins that pulsed, pulsed, pulsed with the reddest of reds. That's how we survived.

Inevitably this mound forgets how to be ashamed. This hypo-ventilating collective: limbs and disembodied heads breastless, a pregnancy without birth. No longer people, we suckle one another. We forget how to distinguish the smell of fresh milk from that of a carcass. There is no other way to keep those left alive but to palm-feed blood to listless mouths with teeth and no speech.

The air grows thick with arsenic and asbestos. The mound goes hush, hush! Knuckles no longer twitch to find each other's grips. It's unclear whether there was still breathing to be heard when particles, paced as they were, expanded within hearts and beat (beat)

beat (beat)

beat (beat) them apart.

Ouse

the river cradled your legs and skirts, riverweeds, sentiments,
paltry pond fish, the freshwater kind, and
the stones diligently piled into your deep pockets —
those fingers must have been beautiful even picked to the roots.

It grows (we decompose)

Under water we are now all blue streaks of planktonic phosphorescence,
all fish colored with bleeding dyes, globular bergs of trans fats separating
from our bodies to push against ex-glaciers that feed
the
    endless
expanses
        of
            waves
        that
    must
always
    stay
            green,
    amen.

Monologue for the Fire Escape

I'm wrapped. I scrape the requisite metal across the palm of the big big
world.

I admit I do require the sweet sedation. You admit you do, I relax, we
relax. Laugh, even, but let's not dwell
it's getting late.
lips alight and me? I'm tamed.
I only hear the calming flame.

The erupting blaze can't be my hell,
at least not when I wear it well.

the text message ends with lol, indicating I was only kidding

This browser tab is a poem. Keyboards are not romantic
and the future is not a romance now. Sometimes
sometimes the processor skips a word the keyboard gets stuck
here, now, sometimes the keyboard gets stuck
and says the same thing over and over again
sometimes I get stuck/I say the same thing over and over again—

have you ever thought about how poets have to tell you the truth
what an excruciating task
telling a page anything is like screaming at a rock to bleed
like trying to bend a wrought-iron attitude;
what will you do in the end if it listens?

they say if you don't make jokes about everything
you're not really alive I was told that if you can't laugh about it
you can't be about it haha I mean you haven't healed,
what's a band-aid when the wound still bleeds
I try to pin down why I am like this
all poets want to know is "why"
so that once we figure it out we can dress it in flourishes –
to keep it un-distinguishable, let us work on being clear here.

ha ha. Clarity. no wonder the boys get mad,
anyone would go mad in here
twisted up like a vine crawling up a mountainface,
spending millennia diving nails-first into a shaggy stone
just to see what someone else saw from the crag's top all along
lol

similes

I do the wrong thing. I exaggerate. I say: do not love me
I say I'm like the thin layer of cold water on a melted ice coffee,
the fat you skim off chicken soup with a slotted spoon.
I say throw me away like a wet coffee filter
I say wash me out, cut me up cut me off cut me out
rip me up like some post-recycled corrugated
'cause I don't want to be here anymore. Take me home
make this home for me.

No one can ever be home unless they decide to be. Neither can you.

I apologize for the similes. I say: I am sorry for
likening myself to the face of a bronzed duck sinking below the pond,
I say in my and all heft there is value.

An incredibly rapid catastrophe

A man I know now is bad (ha)
asked if I knew of any inspirational poems
Inspirations!
Do I ever:
they live in my head
and die there too,
the littlest of confidences in the smallest of coincidences ike a bubble,
pop! You too could feel good about yourself if you just 1) alkdjf;
2) akldcn;ksww 3)kiio
safdfweast;lasdkisdfweq

you too can feel connnnnnnnnnnnnnnnnnnnfident
if you hop on the bike and pedal pedal
pedal the petals are soft like the coat of a lion, pet 'em,
and like everything they too are made of light.
they're alright, they are all right, if we close our eyes we are alright
in the morning, in the dawn, in the evening, at suppertime, when
Being Alright is the aim it's all the same,
what is reality when the angle changes?
the sun is the sun is the sun is the sun is the sun is the sun is the sun
and we grow under the sun and we die under it too.

Nostradamus Blocks the Standing Area (but who'd want to stand next to his spooky ass anyway)

On the M train
a married man
in a hockey hat
from another town
mouths to himself
as he reads a book
on how to survive.

On the cover an active volcano spews magma out as a title,
something like: YOU'RE FUCKED,
YOU'RE ALL SO FUCKED
BY THE IMPENDING ECONOMIC APOCALYPSE
UNLESS YOU LISTEN TO SOMEONE: ME.
Something like that, but terse.
We all think we're the only dinosaur at the pulpit who knows how to
roar at the meteor with a cracked claw.

I fell asleep.
The dream went like this, that I had blood
in both eyes, incalculably blocked
and opaque red like lava and I could not see
any eruption for what it was and the malice
rolled downhill as it always does
and in the end I burned
and our town did too.

But this guy? His sick little open mouth still spits little spits
as it whispers lyrics to the same tired tune,
din-da-lin:
this is the hellish chorus for our timely demise.

PROMETHEUS
SET A FOREST FIRE

Farewell and onto another vicious winter!

Underbrush's autumn eyes have been caught under our feet.
Warblers crack stalks remembering milder seasons,
a storm shrieks renaissance over umber.
So enters Winter through fields of rotten gold.

Rude though it is, the weather is not what ends us. Not the wind
nor the war, no,
Can't touch cruel vagabonds with simply a whimper.
Those zealous winds can just hiss at our necks since we
use our toes to carve last-ditch remarks in the fine-powdered snow.

Words! Inadequate to describe our disdain of such ice: how
we've peeled water-slicked bones out of their joints,
used wind-crisped nails to strip matches bare one by one,
so now just let us sleep for the return of Eden to our lids.

East 4th at 4:00 in the G-d Damn Morning

Tumble deeper yet upon the metal-glazed streets:
brazen hips to sweaty sheets.
Floors stacked high, incense alight,
bodies exposed—
hands scan,
glance, gasp.
Blinds alive, eyes aghast,
we grab our things and head out fast.
No numbers left, no kiss goodbye,
no memories of this—our night.

Let's Get Busy Under The Bombs (So How About That War, Huh?)

To be a dirigible in the star-peppered sky,
to flash neon upon the steel cloud-stabbers set so sta-ccat-oh,
across this city, split the curtains,
part the pink parts and paint on them a purpled patina.

Oh to float, to be omnipresently afloat,
something of note, to shade sprinklered suburbia
in the inimitable sick-thickened Garden State dawn.

Glance up from the parkway, from the turnpike, up from I-95,
up from the pools, take note! And the row house roofs, take note:
A gale dips down like a dancer flat-footed on fire-frosted thickets.

Look: let's miss mooring.
Watch: we mix hydrogen with oxygen,
let's get busy under the bombs.

Lachrymoseying

I'm not a man, baby,
but neither am I this patch of curdled milk ducts you call a woman.
what is the word for this, when you hate the parts
others love you for,
when your own name leaves
a tin can film on your tongue?
My past is when I tried to get ahold of myself,
get a hold on myself,
but even now here I go
slick through my own fingers,
buttered kernels into the pot, pop.
I sprinkle myself with salt
to deafen the taste,
gnash my marrow into a paste
and casserole my innards
into variety meats to serve on a plate: bon appétit.

You Want to Want What Others Want

You want to feed yourself grapes,
wine, kombucha
from the organic aisle,
all with a view from the top of self-care mountain,
you want to have climbed it yourself but
if wishes were fishes there wouldn't be
blue fin tuna depletion,
the seas would bubble
with sulfuric, displaced wants,
the things you baited but
never had enough line for.
You want to have been who you meant
from the very start, want to have known yourself like
not just in the biblical way
in a guest bedroom, you want to have known
at least
the immutable inevitability of having
eventually to piece yourself together alone,
the courage to see such things like yourself
unfold.

The Latest, Greatest Flood

Like an eroded riverbed collapsed into grass
I have waited
longer than allotted to become again.
I have not taken the time away
from windsweep and nightfall
to cake myself into an acceptable site.
I must emerge weathered
or else like any rotted creek, sink my shores
into an obsolescence once flocked with birds.

Once more from the top, this time with feeling

In the park, hot dog in ~~our~~ my hand, and eating and looking
out onto the reservoir in the sunset on ~~our~~ ~~me~~ my own,
boats not going anywhere, ~~we~~—I say, wet crumbs in a bath.
And Lou sings to me that *it's such a perfect day /*
he's glad I spent it alone, because you could only ever touch someone
like a subway pole. I don't ever feel bad about forgetting you,
and the way the light bounced off of the luxury buildings
onto your stupid-ass face, so the sun is warm against my open palms
and I am open to its warmth and I don't have anyone to touch me,
and nobody to keep me closed
and it is a perfect day,
I'm glad I spent it alone.

Sour metal

the price is up, inflation and all, and Mental Health Fact: didja know
they mine its silvery softness from the mantle like you mine patience
from mine. Fuck the market price of shutting my mouth. load up the
trucks and haul ass out the quarry hold on to mounds of sanity in a big
Swiss bank cause what good Patriot wouldn't dig up the dusty ledge
beneath his own feet to have a pittance of gold in his pocket as he falls

Fantasy by Mariah Carey was Playing in the Background When

So agony aunt,
let's say we have a friend,
let's say his name is Glenn or Ben or Mark or whatever, the point is
let's say in error he drank from the bong. Let's just say
he likes fear ;) so he "lets it" be his mistress.

I know what you're gonna say miss aunt, that We've all mistaken ash
for water, don't beat yourself up for the rolling of the tides
and the moon and the stars the yadda yadda like how
some springs the clock bangs while the heater still ticks
and sometimes I cannot remember what the things in my house are for
so they all gets thrown out. Right? Anyway

Let's say there's no point to responding
to the letters in your newspaper column like there's no point
to fretting about leg hair
like there's no point to fear – in the general sense, not in the specific
There are plenty of things to be afraid of
so let's just say Frank is afraid of all of them and the others too.
I am getting off track

This letter should be twenty pages long but instead it's 30 years
so here's the note, Cliff: if you fear life it's going to leave you behind
and running to catch it, well that's just a sweet, sweet fantasy,
baby

We
prinster
a thousand

as if

minds

truth

we may have peace through

The first of the new-born
the polished
can be as w
m

under the mighty hand

for
this world choke the harmful No reason lives to
watch us
bear our trials and lose heart, and go to pieces
if we find
to

overcome
(so) we may
I will not fear what

boldly say content
man shall do to me

the atmosphere like a fever is contagious. we tend to
for tomorrow into
fall into
painting (that we should) be these things the Ignorance
(the heathen) seek reality who cares above, flowers
fails to grasp in we are not to
Surely surrender each day who cares for sparrows will
the hands for them never makes things better his mind for
the one who does
juices injurious
resistance vision and weaken our desire
becloud our

Momentary

I could die in the big-eyed look you give me
for a moment it's all either of us wanted:
not two pretty people in that way but the others, phew,
overflowing
hands and hair
because you know I don't shave.

You call me, the name I ask,
undo my shirt and my chest and I stretch out like a deep breath.
I like the ring of your elastic syllables against my teeth,
strung out long like a laundry line for wet dresses I don't wear.

We bathe
in the damp lamplight of being two people who don't demand
an explanation for the luminescence of a hand
just willing to touch another, our fingers pulled straight
for now

Left:
Talk to me (found lost poem)

Last Will

De-dessicate me when I'm dry, dedicate me a monument to denial.

And to think! We all want to be the one to stand
on the mound of corpses and summit the hierarchy of death.

Pandemic Polemic

Listen to the small howl:
the kettle has been boiled and poured and replaced onto the hot stove.
How could we ever have thought we were more than this,
a whisper, a whistle, a steel urn with enough space for all our longing?

Think about what you really want like it's the entire sun.
Let it boil your empty metal insides when you are cold.

Would you rather set the house on fire or sit empty on the stove?
You, who keeps a lighter in the junk drawer?

What is all this shit?

Left home for a little while and then I came back.
So excuse me, ma'am, but what is all this shit?
I don't mean to sound dramatic but who let this happen?
Who ripped out facades for these plain slate glass windows?
Who gutted these paths like the streets have no bones?
If it's such a house then why's no one home?

I don't mean to sound dramatic (When I get like that, you know it)
but who here said "irredeemable" and swung the scythe into brick
to reap wheat?
Just asking because I'm curious.
Not for the answer,
but for the pause before the swing of the heart's heavy hammer.

Get in, bitches. It's time to actualize.

convert every last one of my nerves until they all believe
in me too: Newly and forever King of Worries
with a crown of gilded thorns I run from my tower, taxed.

No once-impenetrable drawbridge could keep me now!
How could you settle for cowering?!
Your body thirsts to spread itself out in the grass.

Hold your head up high for yourself—
now that's being in love.

I Imagine That a Hundred Years Ago, on the Morning the G-Men Meant to Take the Bank Robbers to the Federal Prison, It Was Brisk and Clear Like a Pastoral Painting

Three hard-hearted men syncopate robbery:
Six spats on the floor with a one-two/two-three,
they walk to the vault with unfazeable glee
knowing full well that they'd all stay free.

The stories divulge – now a gun's meant to pop
and a man's meant to scream, and the hostages drop.
Or the men meant to scowl while they all wield their bats
before each one struts out with a big heavy sack.

Off they would drive, past the sea with devotion,
where each single man could set his ship in ocean
so every keen sailor could sip on the potion,
Where they could each put all their plans into motion –

I get ahead of myself.

Like all folk tales, this is not the whole truth:
that big ol' reliable jammed up in the booth,
and the one-legged teller knew well what to do
when he struck the tall thief with his giant wood shoe.

The shoe hit his head and his head hit a beam and
the blood and the smash made one upsetting scene –
so security swept, if you know what I mean,
and soon there was nobody left to be creamed.

But oh if you listen into the night skies
you may hear the sounds of such agonic cries
to mark the occasion, a tale for all times –
A wave of destruction by now-famous guys.

Sit, Listen (or, Chronologically This Part of Our Lives Was Spent at the Circus or, Campfire Story)

I.

Upon my monster I tied a bow: pink and glittering
to match her eyes. We walk hand-in-paw on the lawn,
lips to maw. Unyielding promises were made, my mistake.
She growled vowels upon my ear, lovers-speak hidden
in the hisses.

II.

I'm nothing if not like a man with his head poised between jaws.

This was mere metaphor until they dragged her to the cage.

III.

We felt the vast distance of thin bars.
Our hearts grew towards one another
across ochre fur and glass-edged teeth
into the rectangular expanse of the future
ahead.

IV.

The rabble gathered, ripped apart
the intentions of her silken syllables

with their disorderly babble blblblblbl!!!!!! wild noises like an animal
like a raspberry, wanting! The peanuts and cotton candy
thrown at my monster,
I couldn't,

V.

Twilight dripped down the sky when I made the guard's lips sipsipsip.
All it took to unsettle the cage was a few hammerswings of heft,
intention, devotion.

The steel we use to keep space between
ourselves is only ever as strong as its dusty rust.

VI.

We waltzed passed the passed-out guard on our way to the forest,
hoping he slept as well as we did that night.

Forensic

Look at the floor! Look at
the undulating mass on the tile,
how it leeches blood, like, behind the grout,
impossible to scrub with a toothbrush, look! It is you
spread across the floor,
even with a good intentions, what a state of immoral pulchritude!
This is the body you tried to bury, your beautiful body, fool,
Tell me this was worth it.

Ornithological Treatise

In the language of the occupiers, since that is what the town speaks now,
the saying goes like this: that if you feel sorry for yourself,
you pity the little bird.

Who pities a bird?
In my most indelicate of moments I envy even a pigeon,
self-assured pomposity of plumage, the way their chests puff out,
they must just love their big ol' titties but *I couldn't be like that*,
I think, *I'm so unlike a bird* and at this height not even like the small ones,
    maybe something lumbering like an emu, like an errant ostrich,
    flightless-ass bird, neck too gangly, beak too big—

What kind of a prehistoric nut is that big, anyway?
What is that bite for? Why do we pretend
that every evolution serves a purpose
when sometimes shit just ends up the way it is
and that's just how things are because that's the way the bell tolls,
the cookie crumbles—see? We have sayings here in America too,
    you can take the zygote out of the Ex-Bloc via plane, via train,
but you can't get rid of the fundamental truth that as it stands,
when my head's on straight?
I'll take arms over wings any goddamn day.

Cosmonaut on the M/R Train

Despite not having packed the suitcase well,
not having furnished myself with single-serving snacks
and small bottles of wine, I have still
spent this many years on these trips around the sun.

Fuck it, unfurl the banner, mission accomplished and let's go home

to have kept foot after foot stepping and grounded
upon a gray rock so callous and calloused,
to have emerged smiling with most of my teeth intact
despite my tongue's machinations, despite a lack
of inspiration, which is to say that if chance
and circumstance allows it any one of us could make it thru
to Saturn's return.

At night we stand on the tallest buildings to be as close as we can
to the stars, to past-tense particulates
flying by our heads at the speed of us telling one another
that "nothing is guaranteed."
    We call it space because it is harder to fear
        that which we've stacked into taxonomical sacks.
It's trite but only because such safely arranged words never reveal
a whole truth: that the only guarantee is eventuality.

So clutch the cracking mountain ledge, little baby grab the rotting tree,
pet your soul only with a hardened hand whose slim temper
will catch us all, knowing even the rats tip-toeing under the electrified
rail for small snacks like fruit slices will get their comeuppance,
and even the flat-footed who stay put upon the platform will pay
for their safety but so will the men who lean too,
we all have to brave it knowing even the eternal sanguine star can't last.

Think about the bomb:

Think about the bomb:
Put enough pressure
on the smallest piece of cell
and it explodes
like a star
and a dead star
leaves behind a little hole
where nothing else can ever be.

Some say it rips time-space an unfixable gash.
It's like that when people die
sometimes.

Look up at the sky telling you an ancient story:
It's so old the landscape's already changed,
mountains carved into canals
canals filled to be paths
paths paved to be roads. It happens up there too,
in the vacuum of space. It happens everywhere.

I'll tell you what a telescope would tell you: that the end
is never really the end, the end is never really The End
it's never ever really the end

When a thing stops; that's just the beginning

The Day The Teenagers on the Train Dressed Like We Did in 4th Grade

It was that hazy see-thru mesh crop top
with the digital print of the Birth of Venus that aged me.
I was like, damn, where'd the time go?
Remember when all of the computers were
supposed to shut down, shit, do I wish they
had done it, shit, do I wish every last pager
and bubble-backed Mac had all gone black
and the clocks had all turned to blink
00:00:00 and :00 and :00 forever
til the light made us sick and we turned off
the boxes
and we threw away the monitors
we piled them high in a landfill with all our
other open embarrassments, and while we
cracked a book we exhaled hard and said
sheesh, we said
shit, that was close, like,
damn, didn't we almost nearly turn our
spines into themselves like a nautilus,
like an ouroboros didn't we almost swallow
our own feet just to spite our mouths?

If you believe the old stories about the sky:

It takes Saturn 10,756 days to travel around the sun. That means you have 10,756 days to get ready for when he wants to swallow you whole.

Relevant symbolic content for the moment, for the right now moment, for the very present

What's the word
for the symbolism of the beloved ship-shaped shore amusement park
going up in flames on the eve of the only blizzard in four years?
Is that cosmic? Caught by fate on the precipice of escape,
who can't relate?

Hadn't visited in years, can't tell the shipping-laned shoreline
from the prefab Playland gangplank anymore, estranged
by decades of frost with a sore that never stops oozing nostalgia,
duh, it's natural to have wounds that won't heal, and *Arson*
would be a bit too on the nose for the shore, I think from
a different metro area, hearing on the news that the salt-water taffy
store up the stairs smelled like a tire as it burned. No,
too childish. What's property damage, gauche as ever,
in this country? Across the long long horizon no one cares
about the backs of man so who's to care about the front of a brick.

Talking about anything brutal on an endless brutal day has no grace.
What good word is enough?
They are all limp on the shore
with that day-old dead fish smell,
you can't wield them like a butterfly knife.

People say they don't wanna hear about it but get this: me neither.

I'm sleepy all the time,
let's just forget how to talk and pretend we don't have any teeth
It's not that I don't love poems
It's just that they're like a crewless ship burnt to a crisp

Part 2 (Okay, the present is now)

Here's a joke I heard from the past: Here I am, weak over
scorched pirate kitsch, forgetting you can't even cry
about fields of XXXXXXXXXXXXXXXXXXXXXX
with so many limbs hacked off the family tree.

What a jabroni to get upset about what amounts to a cloud
the weather changes
the past doesn't
this is the punchline: laugh when you want to cry like, *oy veysmir,
oy mamatchka, nu, eto zje bil nash dom, kyda eesho?*

Ha

what's funnier than one thing happening over and over even
though we tell ourselves no and we tell each other no no no no
with our fingers wagging, pointed, sharp, whatever –
here it is, back to mitochondrial Eve of a womb born to split open.
I mean it, this is where it hurts.
I never mean anything existentially, no.
I'm no baby with hair caught in the water wheel. No,
I mean that it doesn't matter as in life is short—no,
life is long, no, the real rub of it is that
you never know which one it's gonna be

EXT. POEM - NIGHT, OF COURSE, AND THE MOON IS FULL TOO

This is a scene about a poem. It is not a poem itself or rather it is, in that everything is a poem if you read it with enough breath.

> POET
> Just kidding, that's a joke.

Poems need jokes or else no one will read them—just kidding again, but time I mean it. The poet holds up this very poem as they read.

> POET (CONT'D)
> (selfish)
> What is the meaning of this?

The poet is indignant. This is what indignant people ask aloud when they know perfectly well the meaning of this.

> POET (CONT'D)
> For my words to stand so in
> opposition to yours—unbecoming,
> as in I cannot believe what we
> have become here, together somehow.

They sit. That's the singular "they," this is a poem about a poet after all.

They frown they tut and fret and humph in opposition to the page. They place the page on the ground far away.

They walk away.

> They walk far

far away to the opposite side of the page,
as far away from their own poem as they can.

Once they walk far enough away, this paper doesn't look like a poem.

It is so far they cannot read it anymore.

They shout at it from a distance, this very big distance.

> POET (CONT'D)
> (past tense)
> You read about the space,
> or else you listened to me
> tell you about how it has
> many more corners than

usual as of late. You read about the space and imagine the space with the poet far away.

INT. POEM - CONTINUED

In this take if you want it, you got it.

The poet walks over to a motivational poster. They read it aloud.

> POET
> You wanna get it? You gotta
> (MORE)

POET (CONT'D)
    want it.

On the poster a man pumps iron
the poet aspires to pump iron too, like a man
whatever that is
but for this take they wear a dress
a long knit dress,
the cheap spandex blend that makes their ass look good, ok?

They do their best.
We all do our very best!
And some of us do a lot worse than that, too.

Shh, shh! I nearly forgot this is the part where the poet launches into it:

    POET (CONT'D)
    What can even be said of the
    human condition, not in the way
    that all there is to say has already
    been said but in the sense that
    what in general can be said of these
    Deadened masses, as in, didn't we
    already know we're all assholes—if not,
    we weren't paying attention, typical,
    ignoring that the screech of an empty
    answer from this fetid head could echo
    down the middle of Queens Boulevard
    and ricochet off each one of the three
    three-story malls? What kind of truth

are you looking for in any monologue?
What will it bring you? What did you
forget before you left the house that
left you curling your back so crooked
like an old farmer's wife?

EXT. POEM - CONTINUED

See what I mean? I said you didn't want to go there, didn't I?
Didn't I? If I didn't, I should have propped up
another great big warning sign you're bound to ignore.

> POET
> Sorry – we hardly even know each
> other

I don't even know your name. Who am I to say how you feel?

That's what we call projection,
to feed my film straight through your optic nerve and see
it play out on the blank insides of those big wide irises.

Let's watch it together.

> POET
> Let me see what you see. Let me

Peer through those lenses until the last credit rolls.

St. Valentine's Commando, Quarantined

They say on the day Saint Valentine was decapitated his blood ran red
across the marble crimson as the crushed curtains of a Caravaggio.
Now I get emails about how much the brand that sells
the underwear with the slack-jawed waist feels for me.
They say "We ♡ Briefs!" they do not even offer me
a construction paper picture of Bugs Bunny saying "We Love *You*!"
like don't I deserve a little of the romance? No?

No, they offer me 10% off but
I don't need new underwear.
Underwear is for people with things to do
I have nowhere to go
I just am

there is no "under there" – the forecast says
everything is surface level on the frozen lake today
and the ducks tuck their beaks, asleep,
but the alligators we ignore hibernate with their noses above the ice,
bergs waiting to defrost and wake up to bite.

I don't mean it,
I am excited just to be here
I came here to make friends not win
I am mostly excited just to be alive, wow! who couldn't be!
for the era glistening with robocalls with Scam Likely
and automated A/B testing to nail down a subject line
with the exact bit of copy
that'll make me *just cry* for a cotton/poly blend

but Joke's on the copy team 'cause
I only cry at movies now so
Wake up and empty your Promotions folder and take a note to
Spit hopelessly into the sink the last listless bits of contentment:
I am the ruler of my own destiny, or whatever, I whisper
into the mirror to appease the affirmations god as I see fit, I say:
I am happily I am happily I am happily going about my day

Today's Forecast

Like snow,
we all fall
so far up
into the atmosphere,
pulled away by the suns, scalding Earths
with wet gravities unknown
by sonar, to radar, of lasers, these pressures pop our bones free
and no one is worried about being hungry
as we float
back down
descend
to a ground
too warm
to ever
welcome
our
melted
parts
whole.

Flight to LGA

There's no place like a ratty street corner and a luxury tower and a restaurant that's a bank now that will be a restaurant again, it's cool, it used to be your favorite bar that used to be your least favorite bank but that's history, folks! No time to tango through the time-worn ticker tape past when you blow down the boulevard in a tire-worn taxi cab, and know anyway that if you turn back to Sodom for a salty second it'll still never be like the past never was when they come to chip off a piece of the old block.

Good Morning Astral Projection or Whatever

Repeat after me:
I can see the tide turn.
I bow to it. Who'd win?

And anyways like a wave you trust to bring you back to shore,
I know that learning the best gifte truth I vabout you
I know thaljer I meant to lwearn what the ikmt
(I mean I meant to learn the truth about you but it was hidden here.
A receiptless gift I couldn't keep.)

The truth is:
Repeat after me: thank you.
I am so glad to be here, ah,
standing upon a medium-height podium
of softly running sand.
It's a sponge, actually.
It's a a satellite.
It's a saddle.
It's a soft-soft semi-circular credenza sitting listless in the half-pipe.

Ollie-oop over what I was gonna say,
that I live in the high high atmosphere like rain.
That's what keeps the Earth orbiting around the sun:
That everything that once was a memory will be again.

notes

The numbers lie and people do too so
why don't you write a personal essay about the time a spider
crawled up your asshole and died and why don't you tell 'em
how for a few years after that you were a spider too
– but the man giving out pie chart said to just take a slice, so
why don't you write a personal essay about how the teacher
made a kid wait so he went on the red plastic bucket chair and it pooled
all in the middle and he was like fuck the man, fuck it all
and I bet the kids who laughed would piss on what they hate too now
and anyway good luck standing up to a graph at the top of its hill
without a sled, so why don't you write a personal essay about
how you went to the edge of the atmosphere like a conquerer but all
you found was mostly people won't change, write an essay about that,
tell 'em how over time they lose the edges of their shapes
while growing sharp at the formless center

so everyone in the room can laugh until they cry and say "no."

Get this: it's Brunch but in the near-future, near enough
that everyone around you is the same but far away enough
that there are now two competing brands of flying car

We are having lunch.
Nah jk lol we're having brunch, of course,
but we eat it for lunch.
Once you told me that the sun doesn't rise before 5
so you'll sleep in too. Whatever. I'm not yr mom in broad daylight
or really at all anymore, sun notwithstanding.
You'd say the idea's detestable and for once you'd be right.

So anyway now we're eating brunch for lunch and you tell me this,
you say: bitch, how are you. I say I am good (which means I am fine)
You say you are good, which means you are fine, I did not ask.
We are fine, which is good. It is good to be fine. It is fine. It's OK.
We order salads.
Haha we order burgers, I mean, duh? But make mine a double
and *please*
for the
love
of
Gawwwwwd can you pleasepleasepleaseplsplspls
make them crispy this time, the onion rings, please, thankyousomuch!
I wish this vocal fry went even higher but
I say, I wish I was still in bed
and you think that's rude even though you'd never have the guts
to speak a truth instead I have to read it off your stupid
gaspy little expression of which, by the way, I am still sick.

like I already said because I have a backbone

Anyway We do a liiiiitle bitta something out of your man purse. Ha ha,
Old habits dunno how to die

they just linger like an old man on a bench. Same,
I say, haha, it's a good thing your dumb little man-purse
is gender neutral now and you don't say anything about it because you
don't care about the things I say anymore \ because you don't want to
admit anything to one another, which is fine with me,
by which I mean literal lol it's Good actually that we no longer care.
Anyway we are manic so I tell u that the sun was a poet
writing a novel and THAT
haha
get this!
that's why it/he exploded!

You say it exploded because that tiny sun rammed into our big sun
And the big sun was supercharged or a nova or novel-something
And the big sun was tired of pulling along the little sun and they both
just chose to become one big bad black hole. Like we did.

I say jeeeeeeee*eeyuz* lighten up. It was a joke! Stars are just the past.
Light is the past.

And you say: What about the psychic calendar tipping magnetically
against the poles???

How all of the ducks dance in a grim little circle
and all the turkeys dance in a grim little circle
and the hamsters and the hogs and the big fish know how to die
in the saltiest part of the lake, below the deep-dark sulfurous caves.
Haven't you seen that one? You wanna talk real?

No, I say, damn, you're cold, and over the high-pitched laughter,
the Sunday after-morning club music, three juices and the cosmos
mimosas and negronis and lychee nut martinis and cocktail weenies
I think someone at the next table over yells, like:

 "What if we were in touch with the root-toed fruit trees, how the
marigolds who blossom in the golf course get mowed down?
How the mushrooms all touch and talk and how we all don't even
do that anymore?"

We look past each other. You don't talk now 'cause you eat cold eggs.

Huh. I think. Not about how eggs keep you busy but about how
Once the skies were blue, not red, and once,
before I'd learned what it meant to look up,
it had really been like we were almost in love.

Oh, I let the garden go barren in the winter to kill your troops but now that it's spring? It's mine, all mine

Sometimes the light teems with shadow
and the seeds of sunflowers are simply ants, and the people you knew
aren't the people you know anymore
and sometimes you reach for the sky
and sometimes you reach to the ground
and you can't take them with you
the way you can't carry cash into the afterlife
the way you can't hold a whisper in the freezer,
the way you can't keep a cloud in an envelope,
the way you can't un-tell the truth once it's been told,
the way you can't forget this: that the people you loved
aren't those people you loved, not anymore, the way
you can't miss a kiss after it makes a sound, the way
a heavy cloud gives in to the rain,
the way we could not have kept knowing one another
with the wind having blown the way it did.

Palimpsest

What's a body but an echo? You've got your great-grandfather's name,
I've got my thirdhand account of ancestors who smuggled liquor
by boat. The carved words on the gangplank say stupid, brave,
potato, potato
I say in Ukraine there were only really a few ways to say potato
but my foreign-formed body wasn't born overseas.

Life is like a layered coconut cake — no, lives pile on top of each
other compacted by the heavy years, sediment forgettable
like a snail shell stuck in clay
for sixty years but wouldn't you know it?
it crumbles if you pull it into the air — us too, like earth churning
from the core, liquid molting to cool cool rock.

sometimes when I look in the mirror I see my grandmother's eyes
and sometimes when I look in the mirror I see no one at all.
Maybe these are the same the way that fog is the ocean is a stream is
spit in the toilet bowl.

When a building is knocked down for a J.P. Morgan Chase for a
Target for a condo-C Class hybrid — sometimes,
from the parking deck,
you can still see the building's ghost pressed into the brick:

Palimpsest, curled under the Vesuvian ash.
We can all see our skeletons firing under the nuclear shine.
That's what our bodies are: not a sound,
an echo.

About the poet:

Charline (Charlie) Tetiyevsky lives in Queens, where they write film and television scripts and are working on their forthcoming debut novel. Charlie's first poetry and photography collection, *Things to Keep the Living Alive*, was published in 2007 and they released the zine *Rude Flash* in 2015.

The poems in this book were written in New York, Australia, and Los Angeles while Charlie worked as a writer and journalist covering politics, psychedelics, popular music, and pornography. Charlie's essays, prose, poetry, and non-fiction have appeared in many magazines including PRØHBTD, XBIZ, Lambda Literary, Quarto, Tablet, the Susquehanna Review, the Birch, and Collective Presse and they have been featured at readings around the world. They graduated from Columbia University in 2012.